Nail Art

Easy, Creative Nail Art Designs for International Women's Day

Copyright © 2021

All rights reserved.

DEDICATION

The author and publisher have provided this e-book to you for your personal use only. You may not make this e-book publicly available in any way. Copyright infringement is against the law. If you believe the copy of this e-book you are reading infringes on the author's copyright, please notify the publisher at: https://us.macmillan.com/piracy

Contents

White And Orange Flames Nail Art 1

Purple-Pink Floral Nail Art 4

Color Splash Nail Art 7

Colorful Clouds Nail Art 10

Diagon-Alley Pink And Yellow Nail Art 13

Plastic Wrap Nail Art Design 16

White Minimal Chevron Nail Art 19

Striped Aztec Nail Art 21

Pink Ombre Nail Design 24

Gold Glitter Nail Art 27

Smokey Grey Nail Art 29

Chocolate Gold Nail Art 32

Four-Leaf Clover Nails 34

Two-Toned Blue Nail Art 36

Strawberry Fields Forever Nails 38

Deep Blue Nail Art 41

Love Nail Art Design 43

Triple Cloud Nails 46

Scales Nail Art Design 48

Lavender Circles Nail Art 51

Leopard Print Nail Art Design 53

Musical Notes Nail Art 56

Red And White Polka Nail Art 59

Yellow Grapefruit Nail Art 62

Skulls Nail Art 65

White And Orange Flames Nail Art

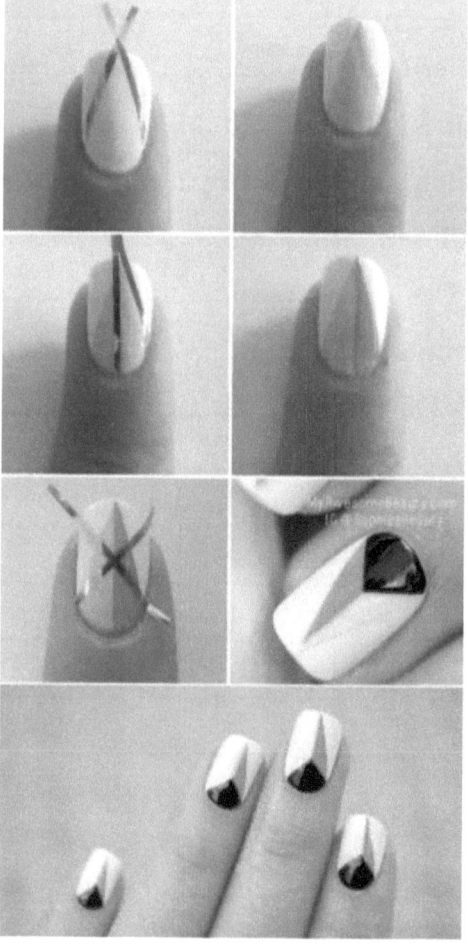

Everything about this nail art design is so fresh and youthful. The color combination is great, and it can be pulled off as the perfect summer nail look. You can also use a different set of nail colors if you're aiming for a different look.

Materials

A white nail polish

Orange nail polish

Yellow nail polish

Black nail polish

Nail art strips

Instructions

Step 1

Apply two coats of white nail polish for the base.

Step 2

Place the strips diagonally across each other and apply a coat of yellow nail polish.

Step 3

Place another strip vertically at the center and apply orange nail polish on one side.

Step 4

Place the strips as shown in the image and apply black at the base of your nail.

Step 5

Apply a coat of clear polish to complete the look.

Purple-Pink Floral Nail Art

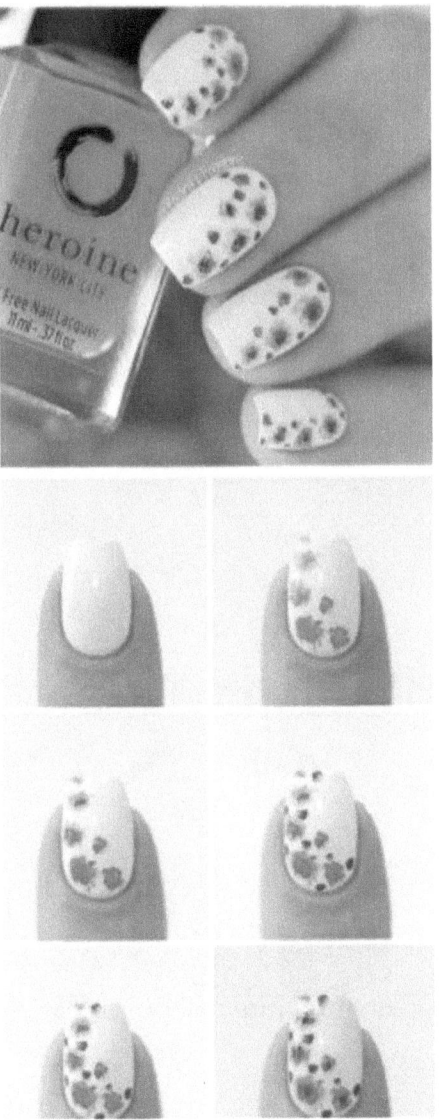

Don't these nails look pretty as hell? The pink and white combination is delightful and is basically like you have spring on your fingernails. It's a simple yet classy design and can be recreated in just a few steps. You can wear it to brighten up those dull days or even on a sunny summer day.

Materials

A white nail polish

Pink nail polish

Purple nail polish

A thin nail art brush or a nail art pen

Instructions

Step 1

Start by applying two coats of white nail polish for your base.

Step 2

Using a thin brush, create the flowers with a pink nail polish.

Step 3

Use the purple nail polish to add some oomph to the pink flowers.

Step 4

Finish with a top coat.

You can choose to recreate this look differently as well by creating flowers on the whole nail instead of just one side. You can also use other bright colors over your white base.

Color Splash Nail Art

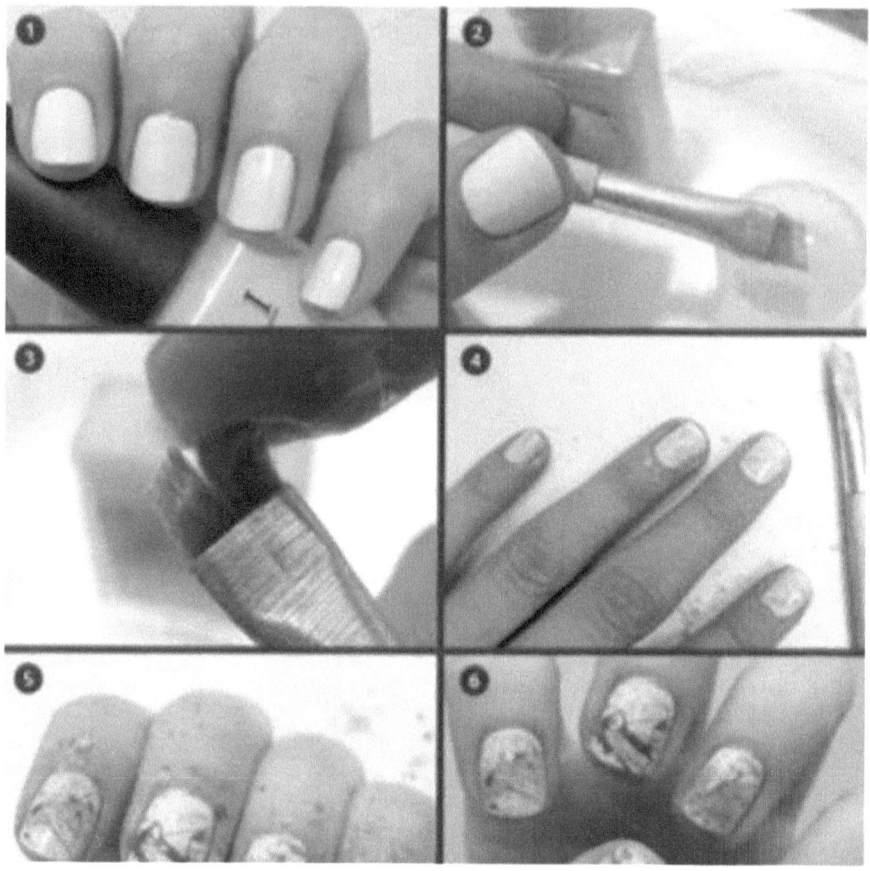

This is by far my favorite nail art design. You are using your nails as a blank canvas and splashing some colors around for that cool effect. Isn't it just so artsy?

Materials

White nail polish

An angled nail art brush

Blue nail polish

Purple nail polish

Pink nail polish

Note

You can use any colors of your choice for this look. It will still look just as cool.

Instructions

Step 1

Apply two coats of white nail polish for a good base.

Step 2

Once it dries, dip the brush in blue nail polish and using your thumb, splash the color over to your nails.

Step 3

Follow this process for each color until you achieve the look that you want.

Step 4

Apply a top coat to set.

Your nails are your very own modern art masterpiece now!

Colorful Clouds Nail Art

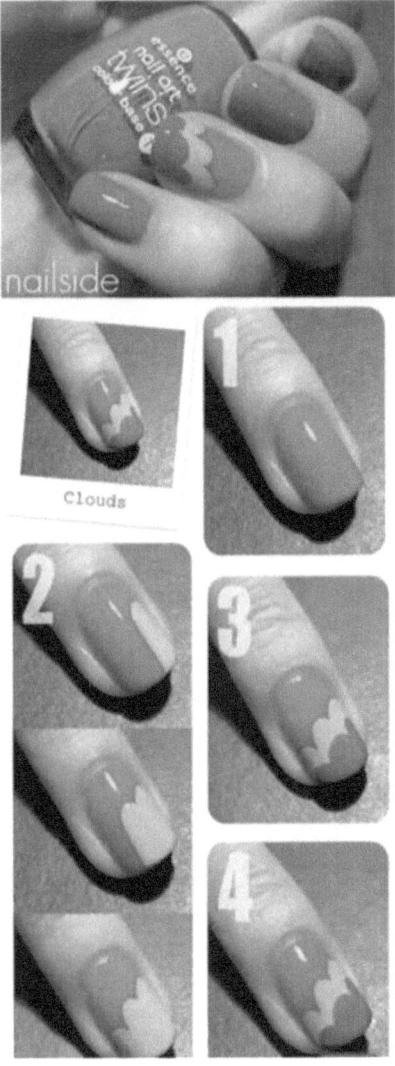

There's nothing to not love about this design. It's colorful, it's easy, it's bright, and it's so damn adorable. We're playing with just the ring fingernail, and the others are left with a minimal aqua green-blue coat of nail polish. This design is perfect for the spring and summer.

Materials

An aqua green-blue nail polish

Pink nail polish

Light blue nail polish

A brush

Instructions

Step 1

Paint all your nails with the green-blue nail polish except for your ring fingernail.

Step 2

Use pink nail polish for your ring fingernail.

Step 3

Use a brush to create the clouds. Start with light blue nail polish and make the vertical lines as shown in the picture.

Step 4

Once it dries, use the green-blue nail polish to create more clouds on top of the light blue surface.

Step 5

Apply a coat of clear polish on top.

Wasn't that simple?

Diagon-Alley Pink And Yellow Nail Art

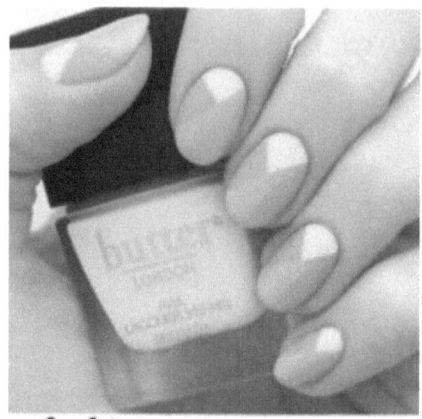

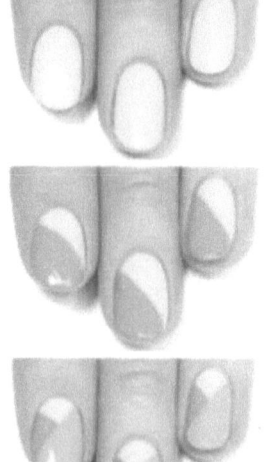

This colorful nail art is a treat for the eyes. It's trendy, vibrant, and young. You can pull it off casually and it will brighten up your outfit and your day!

Materials

Purple-pink nail polish

Yellow nail polish

Peach nail polish

Nail art strips

Top coat

Instructions

Step 1

Start by painting your nails yellow.

Step 2

Paint the lower half of the nail with a peach nail polish, going diagonally across the nail.

Step 3

Repeat the same with the purplish-pink nail polish, going diagonally across the other way.

Step 4

To finish, apply a top coat and you're good to go!

Plastic Wrap Nail Art Design

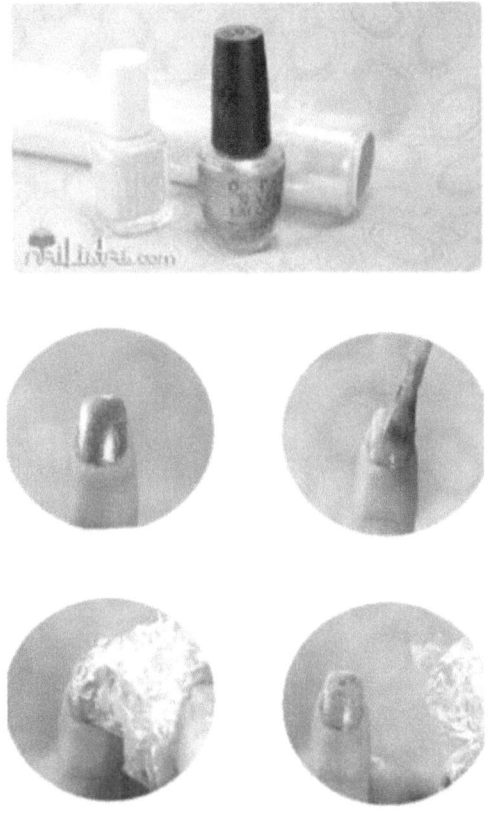

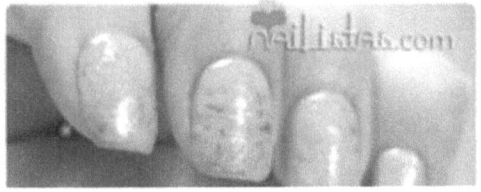

This rare combination of light blue and gold is fabulous. You can wear this look either casually or for a fancy event to go with your gold outfit, perhaps? We're using plastic wrap to get that unique texture on the nail.

Materials

Light blue nail polish

Gold nail polish

Plastic wrap

Clear polish

Instructions

Step 1

Apply two coats of gold nail polish for your base.

Step 2

Once it dries, apply a coat of blue nail polish over the gold.

Step 3

While it is still wet, dab crumpled plastic wrap over your nail.

Step 4

You will see the gold nail polish seeping through the blue; finish with a top coat!

White Minimal Chevron Nail Art

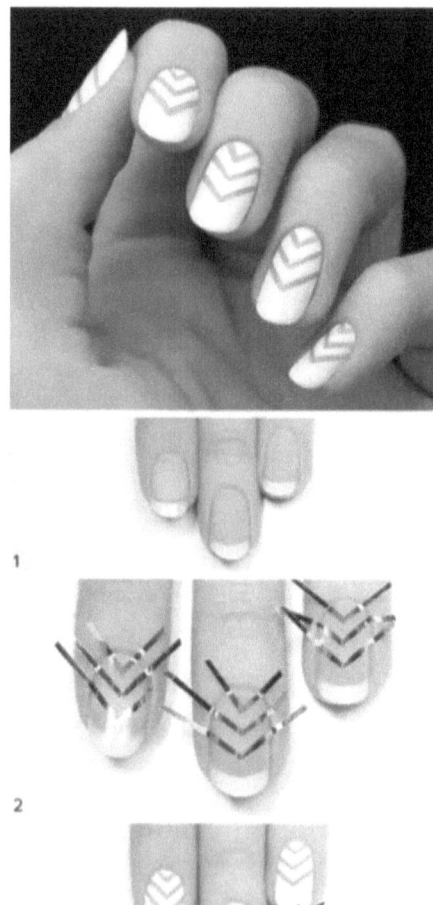

This minimal design is uber classy and simple to recreate. It's all white and anything all white automatically takes exclusive to another level. Don't you agree?

Materials

White nail polish

Thin nail strips

Clear Polish

Instructions

Step 1

Start by placing the nail strips over your nail creating three Vs.

Step 2

Apply white nail polish on the tip of your nail.

Step 3

Use a thin brush to fill in the white between the Vs.

Step 4

Gently peel off the stickers while the polish is still wet.

Step 5

Apply a coat of clear nail polish to finish.

Striped Aztec Nail Art

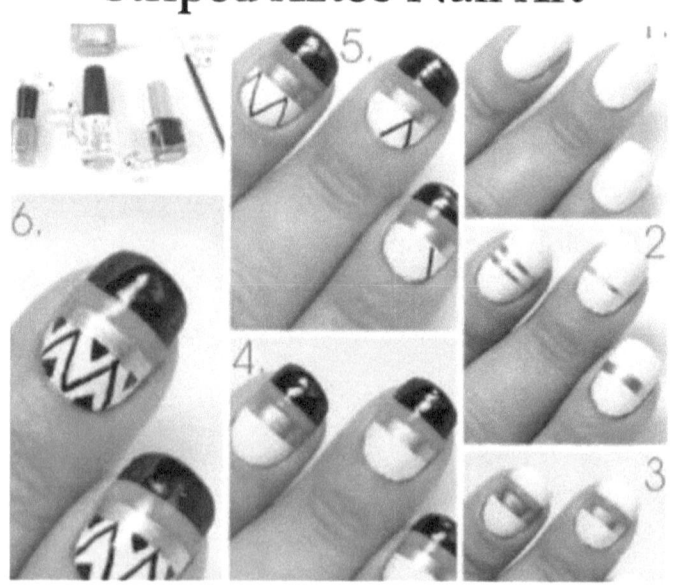

This may look complex but we've broken it down to just a few steps, and you can get this look right at home. It's THAT easy. Isn't it the prettiest design ever? Also, we are totally loving the color combination that's going on. It's so good!

Materials

White nail polish

Black nail polish

Pink nail polish

Gold nail polish

Thin brush

Thin nail strips

Instructions

Step 1

Paint your nails white for the base.

Step 2

Once it dries, use the nail stripes to create the gold stripes with gold nail polish.

Step 3

Next, create the pink stripes.

Step 4

Use the same method and create the black stripe at the tip of your nail.

Step 5

Using a thin brush, create the aztec design as shown in the image.

Step 6

Finish by adding triangles in the middle.

Step 7

Apply a coat of clear polish to set.

Pink Ombre Nail Design

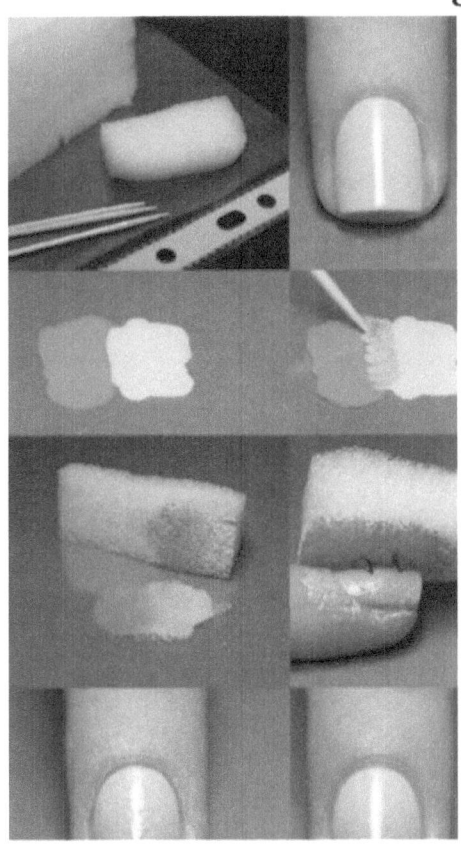

A pink gradient is created to achieve these pretty pink ombre nails. Don't they look super cute? You can use the same techniques with whatever colors you choose. This is a simple technique and can be done in just a few steps.

Materials

A light-peach nail polish

Pink nail polish

Toothpicks

Sponge

Instructions

Step 1

Apply a coat of the light-peach nail polish.

Step 2

Pour a little of both the nail polish colors on a clean surface or a plastic sheet.

Step 3

Using a toothpick, slightly blend the colors together.

Step 4

Dab the mixed colors using a sponge.

Step 5

Gently dab the sponge on the nail.

Step 6

Apply a coat of clear polish to finish the look.

Gold Glitter Nail Art

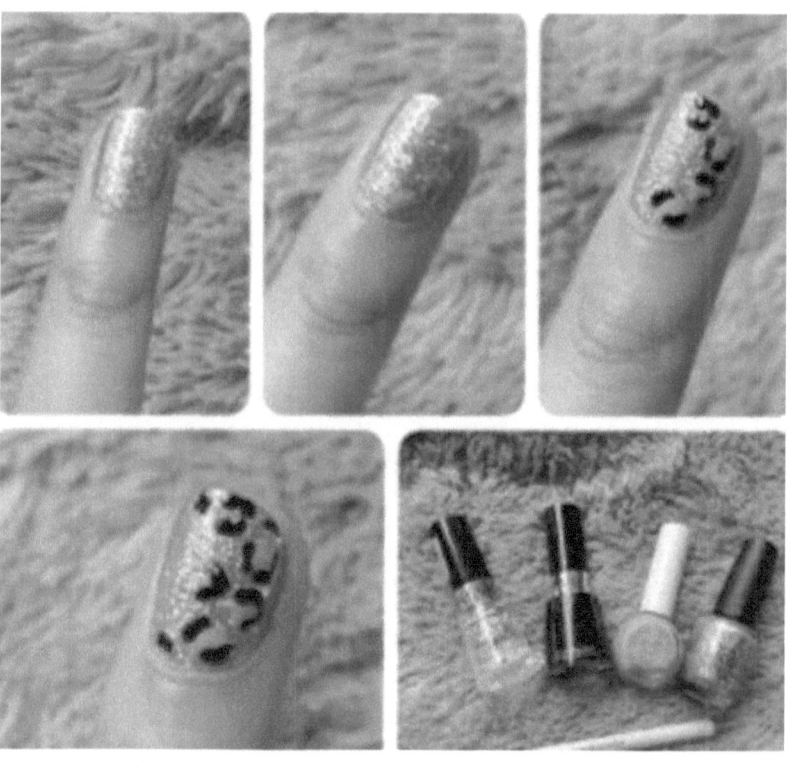

This design is fancy, and it can be worn on days you want to go a little extra! Isn't it pretty? Also, super quick and easy!

Materials

Gold nail polish

Pink nail polish

Black nail polish

A thin brush

Dotting tool

Instructions

Step 1

Paint your nails with two coats of gold nail polish.

Step 2

Create pink dots on the corners with the dotting tool.

Step 3

Outline the pink with black nail polish intermittently as seen in the image.

Step 4

Apply a coat of clear nail polish.

Smokey Grey Nail Art

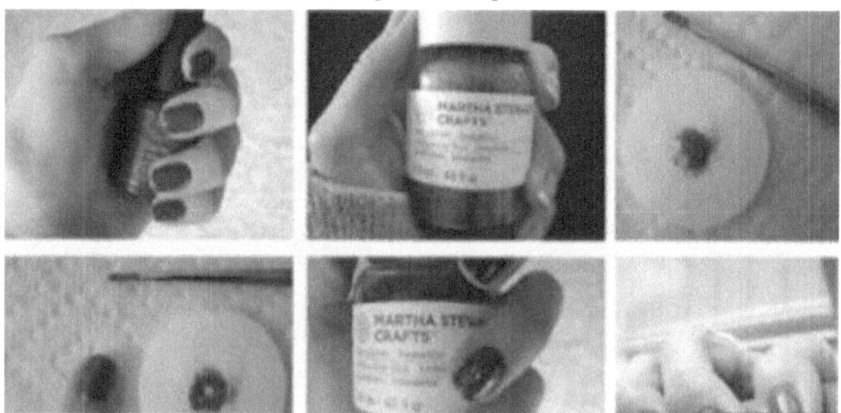

This design is so dark and beautiful. You need to try it!

Materials

A dark smokey grey nail polish

Glitter

Clear polish

A brush

Instructions

Step 1

Paint your nails using the dark grey nail polish.

Step 2

On a clean surface, mix your nail polish with some glitter (you can use craft glitter).

Step 3

Using a brush, apply this to the ends of your nails as seen in the image.

Step 4

To finish, top it up with a clear coat of nail polish!

Voila! Say hello to fabulous nails!

Chocolate Gold Nail Art

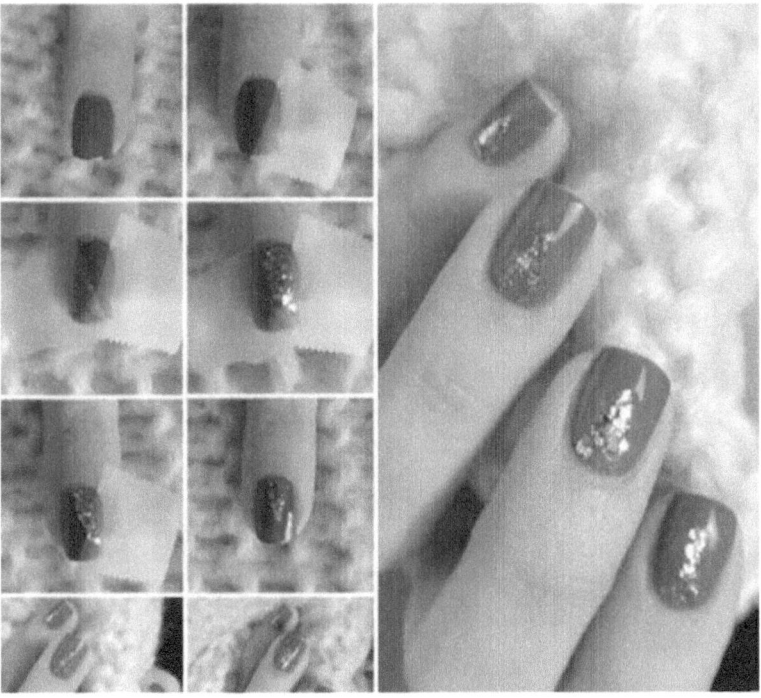

This is perhaps the chicest color on the list. This brown is beautiful, and the combo looks heavenly!

Materials

Chocolate brown nail polish

Gold nail polish

Tape

Instructions

Step 1

Apply two coats of chocolate brown nail polish for your base.

Step 2

Place the tape diagonally across the nail, so as to form a triangle (as seen in the image).

Step 3

Apply gold nail polish in the triangular area.

Step 4

To finish, apply a coat of clear polish.

Four-Leaf Clover Nails

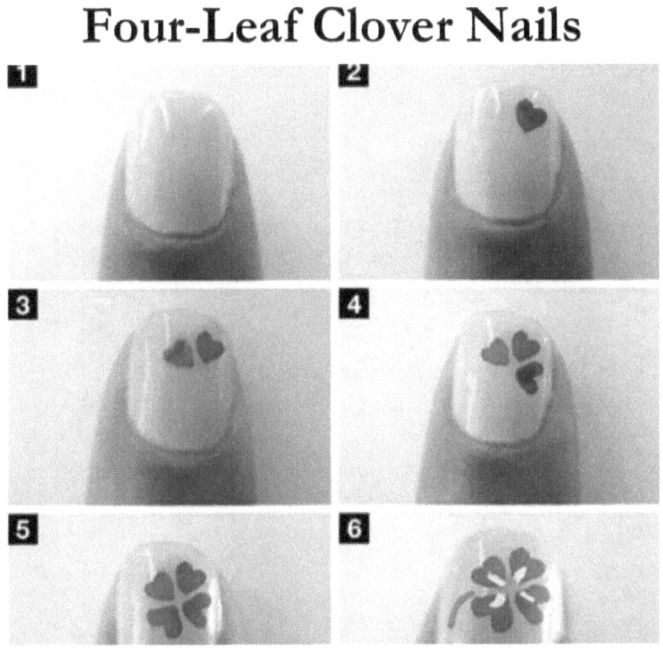

This four-leaf clover inspired nail art design is super simple to recreate. We are loving the pale yellow and green combo. The significance of the four-leaf clover is that it brings you good luck! That's reason enough to try out this design. Don't you agree?

Materials

A pale yellow nail polish

Green nail polish

A thin brush

Instructions

Step 1

Apply a coat of clear nail polish, and you're good to go!

Step 2

Add white strokes to the hearts.

Step 3

Use a thin brush and create hearts as seen in the image with green nail polish.

Step 4

Paint your nails using the pale yellow nail polish for the base.

Two-Toned Blue Nail Art

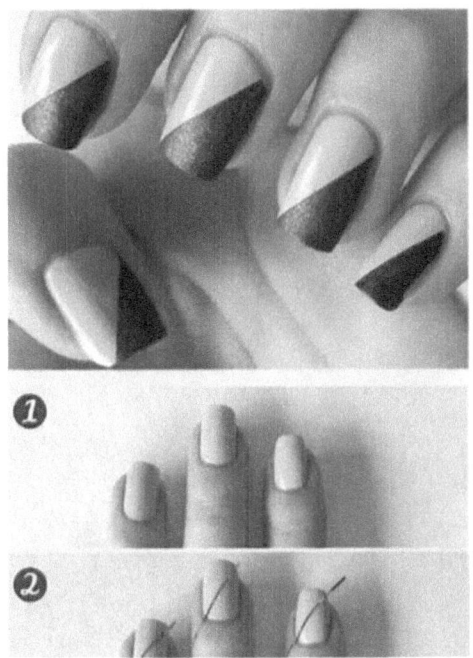

This nail art design is so simple to recreate, and it looks very fresh and classy. You can use any two colors that you like to achieve this look and glam up your nails in a flash!

Materials

A light blue nail polish

Dark blue shimmer polish

Nail strips

Instructions

Step 1

Start by applying two coats of light blue nail polish.

Step 2

Place a nail strip diagonally over your nail.

Step 3

Apply a coat of the dark blue shimmer polish.

Step 4

Top it up with clear polish to set!

Strawberry Fields Forever Nails

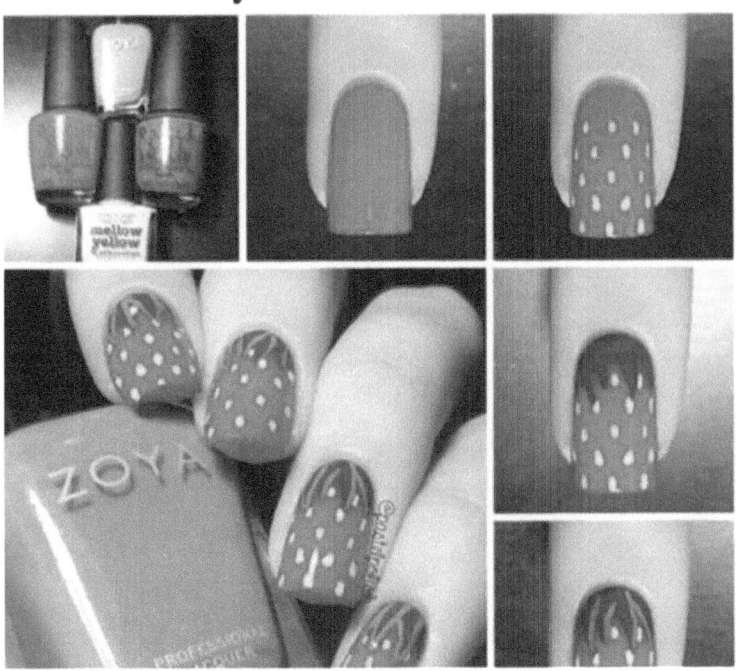

Do you love red but are bored of the classic red mani? Try something different with this strawberry-inspired nail art design. It looks ultra-fresh and can be worn as a fun summer look.

Materials

Red nail polish

Dark green nail polish

Light green nail polish

A mellow-yellow shade or white nail polish

Instructions

Step 1

Apply two coats of red nail polish for your base.

Step 2

Using a thin brush, create dots over your nail with either a white nail polish or a dull yellow shade.

Step 3

At the base, create the head of the strawberry using a dark green nail polish with a thin brush.

Step 4

For a 3D effect, outline the dark green nail polish with a lighter green. This will instantly make the colors pop.

Step 5

Apply a coat of clear polish, and you're done!

Deep Blue Nail Art

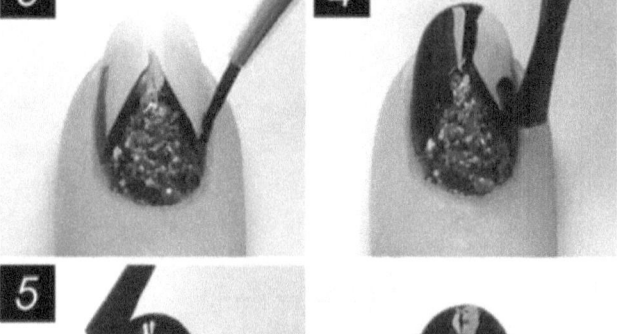

This is a fancy design suitable for occasions when you want to amp up your look. It's also got just the right amount of glitter. You can vary this design with different colors if you wish.

Materials

Dark blue nail polish

Blue Glitter polish

Black nail polish

Rhinestones (optional)

Instructions

Step 1

Start by using the blue glitter polish on the upper base of your nails as shown in the image. You can emphasize on this area using other decorative material as well.

Step 2

Using a thin brush, create a border with black nail polish.

Step 3

Use the dark blue nail polish to paint the rest of your nail.

Step 4

To finish, apply a good old coat of clear polish.

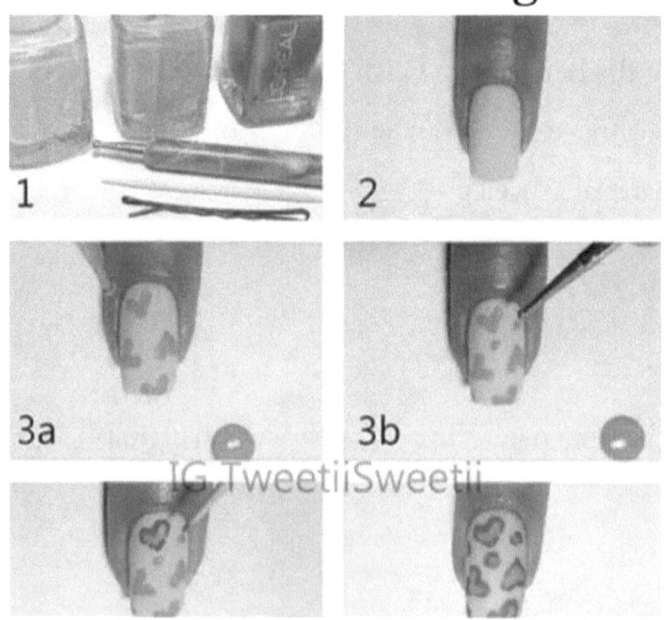

This V-day inspired nail art design is spot on – not too much and just about right. If you're in the mood for some pink hearts on your fingernails, then read on.

Materials

Pink nail polish (3 shades of pink, as seen in the image)

Dotting tool

Toothpick

Instructions

Step 1

Start by painting your nails in light pink for the base.

Step 2

Create hearts using a dotting tool.

Step 3

Use a toothpick to create the borders of the heart with a darker pink nail polish.

Step 4

Apply a coat of clear polish.

Triple Cloud Nails

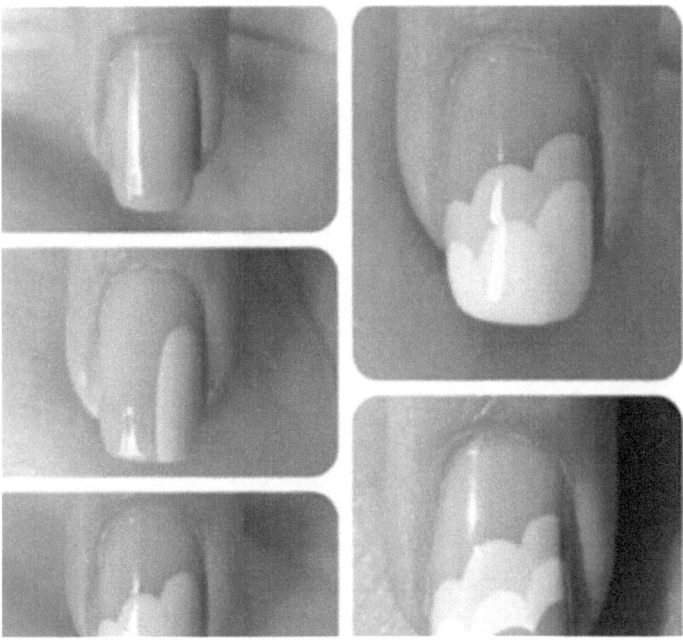

If you want to amp up your regular French manicure, then this design is for you. It's got a very minimal pale pink base and just a few pastel shades of nail polish to go with it.

Materials

Pale pink nail polish

White nail polish

Light blue nail polish

Pastel orange nail polish

Instructions

Step 1

Paint your nails using the pale pink nail polish.

Step 2

To create the clouds, use a brush and start with the light blue polish by making vertical arcs as seen in the picture.

Step 3

Repeat the process with the white and the orange nail polish.

Step 4

Apply a coat of clear nail polish to set.

Scales Nail Art Design

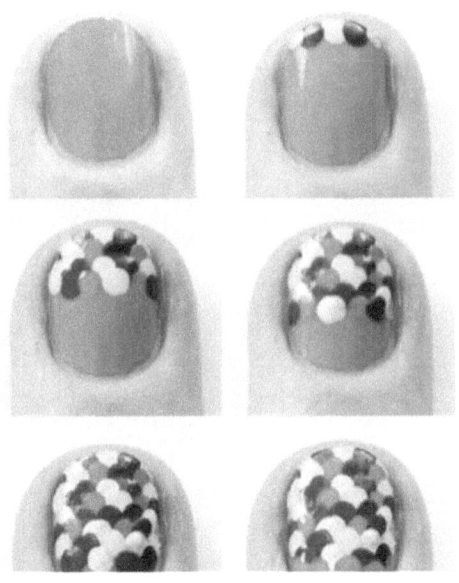

This aqua-green nail art design is literally the easiest thing to do. It also looks great on short nails. It's a forever chirpy color that will make your nails stand out. The color is so bright, and you get to play around with the dots on top using different shades of nail polish.

Materials

An aqua-green nail polish

Beige nail polish

White nail polish

Purple nail polish

Blue nail polish

A thin brush

Note

For the scales, you may use other shades as well.

Nail Art

Instructions

Step 1

Start by applying two coats of your aqua-green nail polish.

Step 2

Use a brush and start at the tip of your nail, creating dots as you go.

Step 3

Move up further until you've created dots till the base of your nail.

Step 4

Apply a coat of clear polish and leave to dry!

Wasn't that super easy? It's for all the lazy girls out there who aren't up for anything too elaborate and are looking for a fun way to do their nails.

Lavender Circles Nail Art

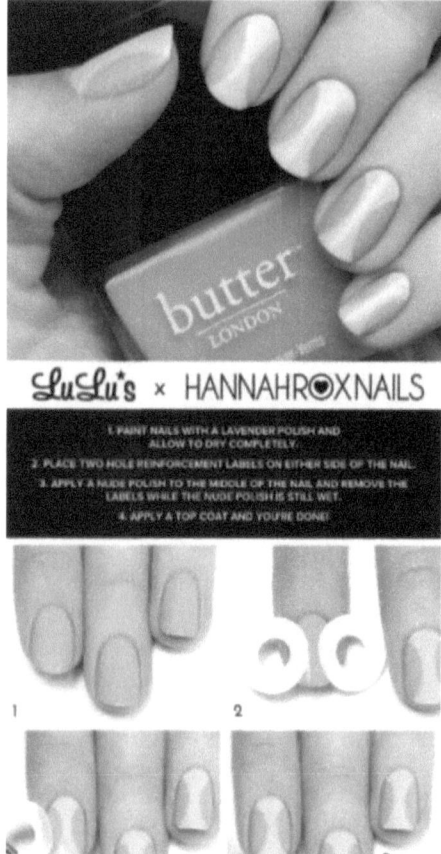

This cute nail art design uses lavender and a grayish nude together, and it's the sweetest combo out there. You can instantly brighten up your hands with this design. Flaunt it in the spring or summer or on a blue rainy day.

Materials

Lavender nail polish

Nude-gray nail polish

Rounded-hole nail art labels

Instructions

Step 1

For your base, paint your nails with a lavender nail polish.

Step 2

Once it dries, place two round nail art labels on either side of the nail, leaving a gap at the center.

Step 3

Apply a coat of the nude nail polish to the middle of your nail and gently remove the sticker while the polish is still wet.

Step 4

Allow it to dry and apply a coat of clear polish to finish.

Leopard Print Nail Art Design

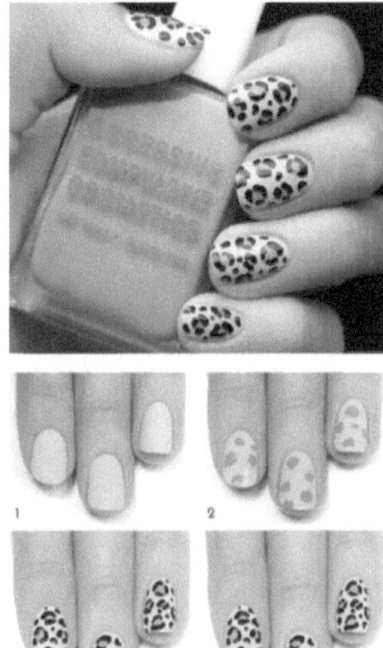

This chic nail art is easy to recreate with just a bit of will and patience. Aren't the end results fabulous? The younger crowd will love this animal pattern and it looks so bold and trendy.

Materials

A nude nail polish

Light brown-beige nail polish

Black nail polish

Nail art brush

Instructions

Step 1

For your base, apply two coats of the nude nail polish.

Step 2

Using a brush, create uneven spots with the brown-beige nail polish.

Step 3

Once it dries, use the black nail polish to outline the spots, leaving gaps in the middle.

Step 4

Top it up with a coat of clear nail polish.

There you go! You now have the chicest nails in town. I'm sure you will get a ton of compliments for this classic!

Musical Notes Nail Art

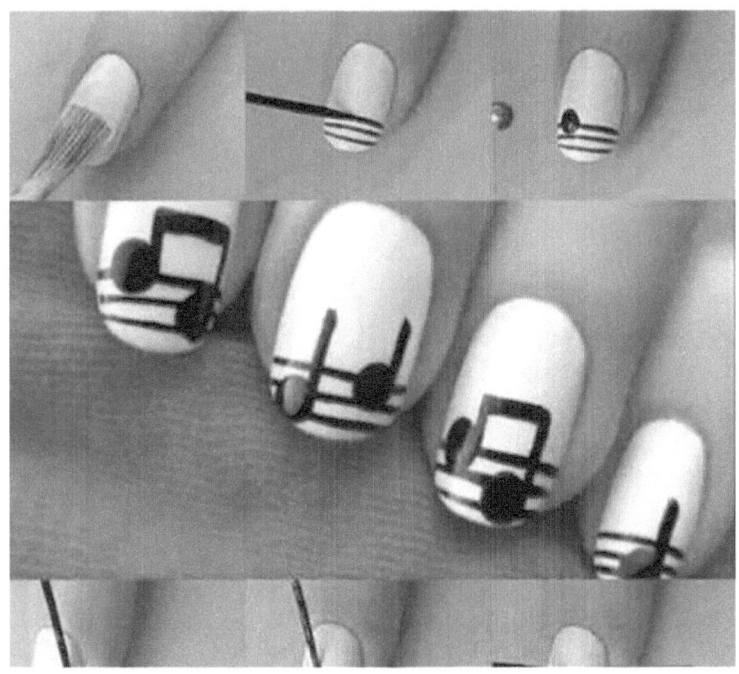

If you're a hard-core music lover, then this is something for you. It's a classic.

Materials

Nude nail polish

Black nail polish

A thin brush

A dotting tool

Instructions

Step 1

Paint your nails with the nude nail polish for your base.

Step 2

Create three thin horizontal lines on the lower part of your nail using a thin brush.

Step 3

Using your dotting tool, create a dot over the lines as seen in the image.

Step 4

Now, create the music note using the same brush.

Step 5

Top it with a coat of clear polish.

Red And White Polka Nail Art

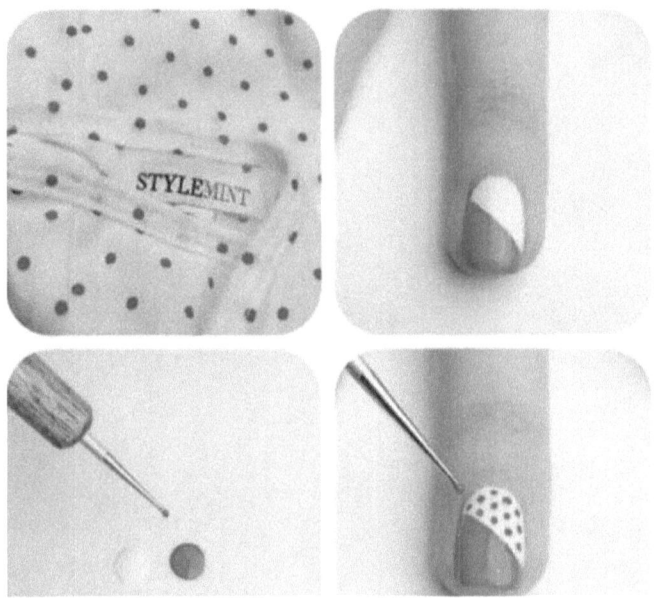

These red and white polka dot nails look adorable! They're so trendy and can be worn casually. You can also use a different color combination if you want to try something different. Follow these simple steps.

Materials

White nail polish

Red nail polish

Nail strips or tape

Dotting tool or toothpicks

Instructions

Step 1

Paint your nails white for your base.

Step 2

Place a nail strip or tape diagonally across your nail and apply the red nail polish.

Step 3

With some red polish on a clean surface, dip your dotting tool or toothpick in the polish and start creating dots over the white area.

Step 4

To complete the look, top it up with clear polish for that glossy salon-like effect!

Yellow Grapefruit Nail Art

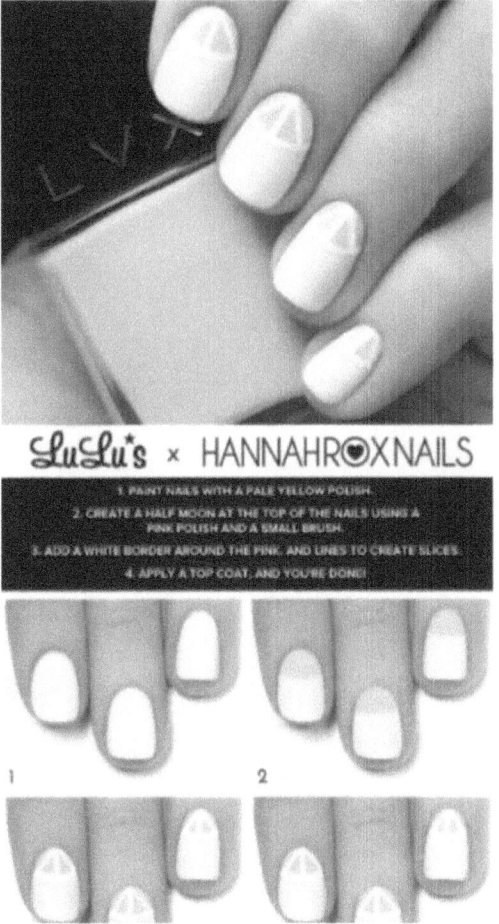

Isn't yellow such a happy color? Some of you girls may feel yellow nail polish is a little too intense, but let's reject that. This grapefruit inspired nail art design is so summery and cute, you just have to try it!

Materials

A yellow nail polish

Pastel pink nail polish

White nail polish

A thin brush

Nail strips

Instructions

Step 1

Paint your nails with the yellow nail polish for your base.

Step 2

Place a nail art strip on the upper-base area of your nail and paint it using the pink polish.

Step 3

Use white nail polish with a thin brush to create the lines over the pink area.

Step 4

Apply a coat of clear nail polish to complete the look.

You can wear this design on your next beach vacation!

Skulls Nail Art

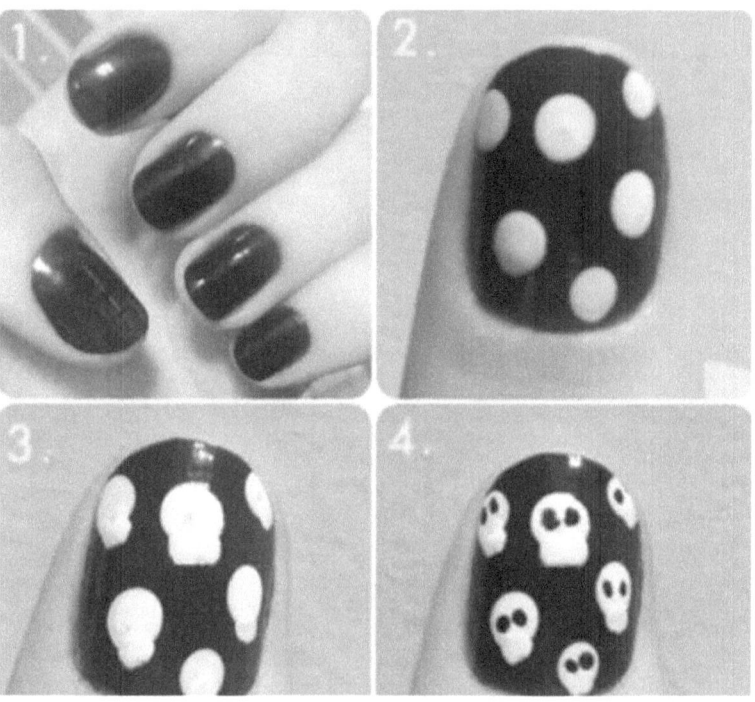

This spooky yet cute nail art design is perfect for a Halloween party! What do you think? Celebrate the fright night with this Halloween inspired mani. Also, it's super quick and easy to do.

Materials

Black nail polish

White nail polish

Thin brush

Clear polish

Instructions

Step 1

Paint your nails in black for the base.

Step 2

Use a brush to create the white spots on your nails with a white nail lacquer.

Step 3

Create smaller dots under the bigger ones to make the skulls.

Step 4

Use black nail polish for the eyes.

Step 5

Boo! Happy trick or treating!

Nail Art

www.ingramcontent.com/pod-product-compliance
Lightning Source LLC
Chambersburg PA
CBHW030458220526
45464CB00006B/2572